**Senses**

Looking and Seeing

Author's Note

I have worked alongside young children for more than forty years. Over this period I have learned never to be surprised at their perceptive comments about the physical world in which they live. Many of their observations ("Have you seen the crinkles in the elephant's trunk?" "How do seeds know which is their top and which is their bottom?") indicate keen observation and an intuitive use of the senses of taste, touch, sight, smell and hearing.

The sense-dependent nature of the young child should come as no surprise to parents and teachers. In the early years of life images provided by the senses shape our interpretation of our surroundings and lay the foundations upon which subsequent learning is built. The ideas of hot and cold, far and near, quiet and loud, sweet and sour, soft and hard are developed through the interaction of the child with his or her immediate environment. This interaction encourages observation and questioning which in turn leads to talk and the extension and deepening of language.

This book (like its companions in the series) is a picture book which seeks to encourage both looking and talking. The text may be read by child or adult. Alternatively it may be ignored, the pictures alone being used to trigger an exploration of the child's own insights.

Published by Raintree Steck-Vaughn Publishers, an imprint of Steck-Vaughn Company, a subsidiary of Harcourt Brace & Company

Editors: Helen Lanz, Shirley Shalit
Art Director: Robert Walster
Project Manager: Gino Coverty
Designer: Kirstie Billingham
Photo Researcher: Sarah Snashall

Library of Congress Cataloging-in-Publication Data
Pluckrose, Henry Arthur.
Looking and seeing / by Henry Pluckrose.
      p. cm. -- (Senses)
Summary: Introduces the basic concept of seeing and how it affects our lives.
ISBN: 0-8172-5225-8
1. Vision--Juvenile literature. [1. Vision. 2. Senses and sensation.] I. Title. II. Series: Pluckrose, Henry Arthur. Senses
QP475.7.P579 1998
612.8'4--dc21   97-30964
                                                                    CIP
                                                                    AC
Printed in Malaysia and bound in the United States
1 2 3 4 5 6 7 8 9 0 LB 01 00 99 98 97

Picture credits
Commissioned photography by Steve Shott: cover, title page, 4, 24. Researched photography: Bruce Coleman Ltd 7 & 13 (H. Reinhard); The Image Bank 9 (J. Humer), 21 (J. Carmichael), 28 (J. Carmichael Jnr); Images Colour Library 6, 10, 12, 16; NHPA 15 (J. Blossom), 18 & 25 (S. Dalton); Rex Features Ltd 5 (A. Griffiths) 17 (K. Andren), 26-27 (The Times); Science Photo Library 14 (R. Planck); Telegraph Colour Library 20 (A. Ponton); Tony Stone Images 11 (R. Wells), 19 (N. Parfitt), 29 (A. Wolfe); Zefa 8 (Eckstein), 23 (Krahmer).

Senses

Looking and Seeing

by Henry Pluckrose

RSVP

RAINTREE
STECK-VAUGHN
PUBLISHERS

The Steck-Vaughn Company

Austin, Texas

4

We use our eyes to see
the things around us.

We see things that
move quickly and
things that stay quite still.

We see the slow,
dreamy movement of clouds,

and the sudden explosion
of fireworks.

We use our eyes to see
bright colors
and soft shadows.

Our eyes see
shapes and patterns –
on the wings of a butterfly
or the scales of a fish.

We see color and pattern
on living plants,
and on the surface of
lifeless brick and stone.

Our eyes can see
things far away
and things
that are close.

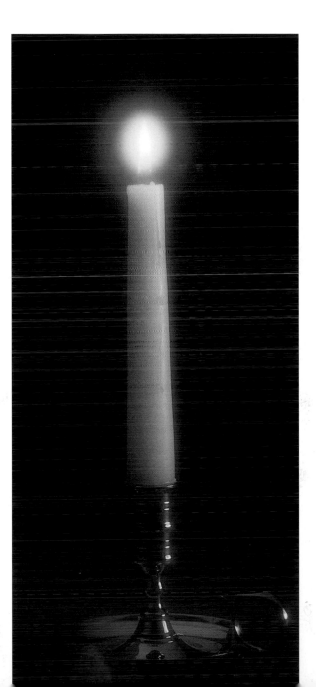

We can see things that are tiny
– and things that are large.

How well do you use your eyes?
Have you seen frost
on a spider's web,
or the delicate marks
on a seashell?

Have you noticed reflections
that dance on water,
or the silvery-blue shadows
of moonlight?

Sometimes things are so small
that our eyes cannot
see them clearly.
We may need a special glass
to make these things look bigger.

Often our senses work together.
Our eyes take messages
to our brain. We see the pig.
We may hear and smell it, too!

Nearly all living creatures can see. But some creatures do not want to be seen. They have colors and marks that let them disappear into the background. This is called camouflage.

Without the sense of sight
we could not see.
Our world would be dark.
We could not see movement
or color.

Investigations

This book has been prepared to encourage the young user to think about the sense of sight and the way in which we use our eyes. Each picture spread creates an opportunity for talk. Sharing talk with a sympathetic adult plays an important part in the development of a child's understanding of the world. Through the subtlety of language, ideas are formed, questioned and developed.

The theme of sight might be explored through questions like these:

⭐ Quick and slow (pp 6-9). What is the slowest movement we might notice . . . a sunflower turning its head through a day toward the sun? A snail crossing a concrete path? What things break suddenly from stillness to movement . . . a cat dashing across a road, a plane on a runway?

⭐ Colors (pp 10-15). What is red? How many different shades of red can you see around you? Are all reds (or blues, greens, yellows . . .) the same? How does a color change when it falls into shade? How do we use colors in everyday life . . . what colors do we use for mailboxes, fire engines, traffic lights, ambulances? Why have these colors been chosen?

⭐ Detail (pp 17-25). Our eyes can see an infinite number of images - far away and near at hand. Why does an object that is large (like an airplane) look tiny in the sky? What fresh details appear when we examine a leaf or a piece of string under a magnifying glass?

⭐ Unity of senses (pp 26-27). It is important to provide opportunity to talk about the way in which our senses work together. What things do we know without seeing? (E.g., the smell of fresh bread leads us to the shelves without first seeing it.)

⭐ The world of nature (pp 28-29). Animals, too, need sight. How do animals use their eyes . . . for hunting, to watch for enemies, to find food? Do all living creatures have eyes that look forward (like ours)?

⭐ Blindness (pp 30-31). Sit with your eyes shut tight. Imagine. What would the world be like if you could not see?